Ten Waves of Awe

Dive Deeper With God and Uncover Hidden Treasures

Mirjam Johnson

Dedication

To God, my Father;

Jesus my Savior and friend;

and the Holy Spirit, my Comforter.

Without You I am nothing,

I am forever Yours.

"Deep calls unto deep at the noise of Your waterfalls;
All Your waves and billows have gone over me.
The Lord will command His lovingkindness in the daytime,
and in the night His song shall be with me-
A prayer to the God of my life."
Psalm 42:7-8

Mirjam Johnson

Contents

Introduction   VII

Prologue   XI

1. Wave One   1

2. Wave Two   7

3. Wave Three   13

4. Wave Four   20

5. Wave Five   29

6. Wave Six   37

7. Wave Seven   43

8. Wave Eight   50

9. Wave Nine   56

10. Wave Ten   65

11. Ten Waves of Awe   70

12. Epilogue   74

13. To the Jewish Reader   77

14. Appendix A   81

15. Appendix B   85

16. Appendix C   89

17. About the Author   91

Introduction

Greetings, peace, and grace to you in the name of our Lord Jesus Christ!

I don't know if it has taken anyone else this long to write a book, but I have been brooding over this book for seven years. And it's finally here! Thank You Holy Spirit!

From the day I was born till the day I wrote these words, I have always been fascinated with God. My mother had named me Mirjam because that name kept coming to her mind while pregnant with me. The reverend of the church explained to her that Mirjam meant, 'Beloved of God'. So, I believe it was God's choice to call me His own.

When I was a young girl, I saw visions and I have memories of being in Heaven. We attended the Dutch Reformed Church. I would ask elders questions about the Bible and they would tell me I was very wise, but could not answer my questions. I wanted to know who God was, and why we no longer celebrated the Feasts in the Bible. I wanted to know how His Kingdom operates. I got very few answers from the people around me.

I remember when I was thirteen, I read my first French book called Jeanne D'Arc. Her heroic story was forever grafted in my soul. I went through our Church Catechism classes faster than others. Therefore, by the age of seventeen, I made my confession for Christ on a Pentecost Sunday. I was hoping for a Divine experience. But we were no Pentecostals and the Holy Spirit was far to find. Instead of experiencing God, I fell into a depression. Many years of trouble began in my life. I started to live like the world does, and it didn't avail of anything but heartache. I was a good student and finished College by the age of twenty-two. I worked in several Laboratories, yet it wasn't giving me the fulfillment that I hoped for. However my life started to change when I took a trip to Israel one day. I saw Jews, Muslims and Christians living for their faith, it was a completely different world to me. I felt God was drawing me closer, but it took me a few more years to completely surrender to His call.

Following Jesus has been the best decision I ever made in life. This book is one of the fruits of it. I hope it tastes sweet to your soul and awakens your spirit. The Holy Spirit helped me to write it all down. Without Him there is no life, no joy, and no strength to live for Jesus. It is an easily made decision to follow our Savior, but it is not an easy life.

Years ago, I saw a book in a church library called; "The Hidden Treasure in Suffering." It was written by Basilia Schlink, a Protestant nun. Honestly, I was kind of offended when I read that title and said to myself, "Well, I'm not going to read that!" But the Lord kept drawing me to that particular book. No one chooses to suffer. But if you wholeheartedly follow Christ, it will find you. God used Mother Schlink's book to prepare me for what He was going to ask of me.

Radical obedience to Christ means overcoming the fear of men, the ridicule of men, and being despised by men. False accusations and religious traditions of men make one look like an outlaw. The good news is, my book is not about suffering. It is about the Divine life in God we can live here on earth. I have added some of my personal experiences and testimonies. Stories that God wrote- to show you how He walks and communicates with His children.

My prayer for you is that you will walk in the fullness of your calling in Him, and be inspired and empowered by the Holy Spirit. That you will find the courage and faith to be who God called you to be.

With love and blessings in Christ Jesus, our Lord,

Mirjam Johnson

Prologue

God's story is a love story. His love runs through all dimensions of creation. To our understanding, love usually relates to our feelings. In God's language, however; it is life. It's who He is and how He operates.

God is also a mystery. We know Him from the Bible. We know Him from our relationship with Him. But then there are times where He seems to hide. We don't understand His ways. We don't see His hand in our life. We become like little children crying out, "Abba Father..."

In the Hebrew language, the word for jealous is the same as zealous; *Qana*. It describes a deep emotion, a feeling of envy and passion for the ones He loves. That has been the story of God and His people throughout the ages. When His people went after other things, other gods, and forgot about Him, He would be jealous. He would send His servants, the prophets, to call them back to His heart. His heart is passionate about His people. To most people's perception, God is impersonal, distant, and perhaps even stern. But that is far from the truth! Thanks be to Jesus, and the Holy Spirit we can be close and intimate with God. Jesus revealed God's love to us. He prayed for you and me;

"O righteous Father! The world has not known You, but I have known You; and these have known that You sent Me. And I have declared to them Your name, and I will declare it, that the love with which You loved Me may be in them and I in them." John 17:25-26

God wants His love in our hearts. That way we know who we are and can show the world who He is. What a marvelous concept of the Father! Paul quotes to us the words from the prophet Isaiah, to make his point.

"Eye has not seen, nor ear heard, nor have entered into the heart of man the things which God has prepared for those who love Him." But God has revealed them to us through His Spirit. For the Spirit searches all things, yes, the deep things of God." 1 Corinthians 2:9-10

Would you like to know what God has prepared for you? Have you longed to go deeper into the Kingdom of God, searching out the riches you have in Christ? Then come with me on a Holy Spirit 'journey' that will take you through waves of God's love. He is zealous for you! I pray that you will be in awe of Him again and again. I pray God will open the doors in your heart to receive more of His love, understanding, revelation, and strength. I hear the Spirit of God saying to you;

"Yes, I have loved you with an everlasting love; therefore with lovingkindness I have drawn you." Jer.31:3

Wave One

Hearing God's voice

"The words that I speak to you are spirit, and they are life."
John 6:63

Hearing God's voice is needed to follow Him. We have general guidance through the Scriptures on how to walk in God's ways. But there are times we need to hear His voice to be redirected to the right place or the straight path. Jesus said, *"My sheep hear My voice, I know them, and they follow Me." John 10:27* I will tell you how I heard His voice in my own life. When I was in my late twenties, I was traveling in the Middle East. Sometime before that, I had left a Humanitarian Aid job in former Yugoslavia. That country was still in the aftermath of the Balkan war.

Working with traumatized children and widows left a deep mark on my soul. I was also dealing with a broken relationship. I had been a Christian all my life, but my heart was very wounded. I had fallen into a deep dark pit that I could not escape from. Call it depression. I saw no purpose for myself anymore and felt that God had abandoned me. I spent a week in the Sinai desert, trying to get myself together. But whatever I tried, failed. I remember I cried every day and found no comfort. I was staying in a small coastal village, where local Bedouins run some guesthouses. Finally, I decided I would cry out to God in the desert. I went for a long walk, wandering away from the village. I was so desperate to meet God that I thought death was the only solution. So I cried and cried and fell on my knees, begging God to just kill me. I had enough faith to believe God could just let a rock fall on my head and that would be it. I was as dry as the desert itself. But then something supernatural happened! An eagle-type bird appeared high in the sky, and all of a sudden wind came rushing around me, like a whirlwind. Then an incredible sense of peace came over me and I heard a sound voice saying, "Because you don't see Me, it doesn't mean I'm not there!" That was the very first time I heard God speak to me, like in thoughts. Then as if I was held up in both arms, I was put on my feet and started walking. I know now that God had sent His Angels to help me. I walked very purposefully to someplace in the vast desert but I didn't know where. Then all of the sudden, I saw a stone Well. Yes, it was a very Biblical scene. I looked inside the well, there was no water in it, just darkness. And then I could hear my thoughts, "That's like my life, I am at the bottom of this deep dark pit and I can't get out." Again, I heard God speak very clearly to me, He said, "You have never stretched out your hand to Me to take you out!" That was the revelation of my life! I knew God, I knew Jesus, I knew the Bible. But I never realized that I needed a Savior! You see, I had always been very blessed and self-sufficient. I was also the courageous kind, and all that brought me very far. But I couldn't save my soul. That experience in the desert changed my life forever. It was as if my heart had opened up and I could speak out my hurt, pain, and struggles. I was so stunned by this whole encounter with God that I couldn't speak for a day. I went back to the Bedouin village, got my notebook, and wrote it all down. A few days later I left the village and went to Cairo, where I happened to meet a believer in Christ from Nigeria. I had a little travel Bible in my native language, but she gave me an English Bible. I started reading it and could not stop. The Spirit of God just washed me over with the Word of God. It was an amazing Divine experience that lasted for weeks. At the time I went to an Arabic language school. I would sit on a city bus packed with Muslims, and still read my Bible. I could not think of anything else than the Word of God. One day I read Jesus' words about being born of the Spirit. I was reading it with my new Nigerian friend at the table. I read it and something fell from my eyes, knowing that I needed what Jesus said. I jumped up from my chair and said," That's what I need, I need a new life!" She was laughing and said she would pray for me. She prayed in her passionate African way and the Holy Spirit came on me. I wept and wept and saw a vision of the Father in Heaven holding out His arms. It was a true prodigal daughter story. And till this day I can still cry about it when I recall it. Surely, I came home that day! The writer of Psalm 95 says, *"Today, if you will hear His voice: do not harden your hearts, as in the rebellion..."* I didn't grow up with the knowledge that God is very personal and wants to be close to me. But from that powerful experience, I learned that I can hear God speak to me and guide me where I need to be. I started to follow

Jesus from that day on and became an instant Evangelist to anyone who wanted to hear about Jesus.

God speaks to us in so many ways. I will not attempt to describe every way God speaks to us, because I would fail. There are at least forty different Bible verses about hearing God's voice. Most Christians agree that God will speak to us through His written word. God also speaks to us through His Holy Spirit, His prophets, visions, dreams, signs, wonders, Angels, and creation, just to name a few. God is Spirit and we exist as a body, spirit, and soul. It's a mystery, but Paul tells us in Ephesians 2:6 that we *"sit together in Heavenly places in Christ Jesus."* God can speak to our spirit that is in Christ Jesus. It is often perceived as heart knowledge. You just know in your heart that you should do something, or not do something. David, in Psalm 139 writes, *"How precious are Your thoughts to me, O God! How great is the sum of them."* God speaks to us in our thoughts. When we learn to discern His thoughts towards us, we hear His voice ever so clearly!

How about you? Have you heard God's voice speak to you? One of the Holy Spirit's names is The Comforter. When God speaks to us personally it's comforting. It's life-changing. "His rod and staff, they comfort me." David wrote. We need our Shepherd to lead us in the straight and narrow path, where His anointing flows and His goodness abides. Let's pray with me.

Prayer time: "Lord Jesus, thank You for being my Good Shepherd. I want to follow You where You lead me. Help me to hear Your voice. Teach me Your way, O Lord, and lead me on a smooth path because of my enemies. Draw me closer to You, so I can know Your thoughts of hope and future over me. In Jesus' name, I pray. Amen."

Faith by works: It's all about a heart-to-heart relationship with the Father. Life's duties, distractions, and perhaps our religious practices are often standing in the way of hearing His voice. We need to escape to the mountain with Jesus! Take some time each day to silence all other voices and wait for Him to speak to you.

Wave Two 🌊

Finding Faith

"When the Son of Man comes, will He really find faith on the earth?" Luke 18:8

I would like to share a story that God wrote in my life. He did this to teach me to trust Him and have faith amid impossibilities. One season, while living in Israel, I was studying Hebrew at a language school. The Lord had told me to go to Jordan. You can cross the border to Jordan or Egypt in the south of Israel. I had been in Jordan years before that. But the difference now was that I had no money for such a journey. I used to support my Missions by working half the year in Holland in the Hospital. I would save up my money and live very frugally. But this time all my money was gone and God did not permit me to go back to Holland. Instead, He told me to go to Jordan! I needed that trip because I was on a temporary visa and I had to finish my Hebrew class in Jerusalem. I had calculated that I needed about four hundred and fifty shekels for the trip. The equivalent of a hundred US Dollars in those days. I'm sure that doesn't sound like much to you, but to me, it was a small fortune! I lived on a budget of about five dollars a day. So, I began to argue with God, telling Him I couldn't go because I didn't have the money. He said," You will go to Jordan." I prayed on my knees probably three, or four times a day. "But how am I going to go, Lord?" What am I supposed to do?" I felt I should simply take steps toward the journey. I knew people who lived in the border town of Jordan and asked them if I could come to visit that weekend for two nights. I realized I needed some sort of proof that I was attending Language School in Jerusalem. In the Middle East, if you travel alone, you are generally deemed suspicious by border security officials. Therefore, I went to the Office of my School a few days before my departure and asked if they could print out proof of my enrollment. The office lady asked me for my ID and I gave her my Passport. She was looking at the computer when the phone rang. She switched from speaking Hebrew to English, saying, "Who are you looking for?" Then she looked at the Passport that was in her hand and said, "Oh, she is just standing with me here in the Office!" Then she handed me the phone. I put it on my ear and heard my friend from the USA talking, saying; "Mirjam! There is 450 Shekel for you at the Bookstore with Benjamin. Go get it!" I was stunned! The glory of God filled that room! His Angels had brought me the provision needed when I needed it! I ran back to my Classroom. Mind you, my class was full of immigrant Jewish people and Arab students, who all needed to learn the Hebrew Language. I had one Catholic friend, who happened to be a nun. I ran to her and said, "God did a miracle! God did a miracle! I told her the whole story, and everyone in that classroom was listening, as the glory of God was so strong! It was an amazing climax after weeks of laboring in prayer, battling fears and doubts. The backstory is that my American friend was on Summer break from the School she was teaching at in Jerusalem. She had told her friend in Texas who I was and how I lived by faith and so on. Then one night her friend woke up and said to her, "Your friend in Jerusalem, I was praying and felt she needs money. And she needs it now!" Knowing I didn't have a cellphone or computer, the only way to reach me was by calling the Hebrew School. It was around 1 am when they called the School from the U.S. It was 9 a.m. right before my class started. God is amazing! *"O you of little faith,"* Jesus said to His disciples. As His disciples, we are always learning to trust Jesus in the middle of the storm.

A few days later I was on the bus to the South of Israel. I could pay the fees and walk across the border into Jordan on foot. There was no one else when I was walking across. It's a typical Middle Eastern desert setting. I felt great and so happy, knowing God was on my side. When I reached the Jordanian side, I saw the border officials with their red keffiyeh headcovers. They are super friendly people and gave me a big royal welcome. When they heard my name was Mirjam or Mariyam in Arabic, they even started singing for me. It was the joy of the Lord and His faithfulness that brought me across that border. It is forever marked in my book in Heaven. That experience propelled me to trust God in greater ways. I hope and pray it builds your faith today!

Faith comes by hearing the Word of God. We build our faith in God by reading and hearing His word, the truth.

When we know the truth and God's will for our lives, we can build our faith in Him. Faith is closely related to trust. We believe Jesus will return and put our hope in Him to save us. But why did He even make the above statement about finding faith on the earth? I think for all of us, faith in God is a challenge. When I want to have faith in a particular area of my life, I find myself in a battle about it! Having and keeping faith in God for answered prayers is laborsome! Jesus was making this statement after sharing the parable of the persistent widow. God does not want us to give up on what we ask Him. Jesus also said, *"If you can believe, all things are possible to him who believes." Mark 9:23*

The writer of Hebrew says, *"without faith it is impossible to please Him, for He who comes to God must believe that He is, and that He is a rewarder of those who diligently seek Him." Hebrews 11: 6*

What is it in your life that you have been praying for, believing in God? The beloved disciple of Jesus wrote the following; *"Now this is the confidence that we have in Him, that if we ask anything according to His will, He hears us. And if we know that He hears us, whatever we ask, we know that we have the petitions that we have asked of Him." 1 John 5:14-15*

Prayer time: "Faithful God, thank You for being with me all my life. You never leave or forsake me. I know You want to bless me and help me trust You in greater ways. I bring all my burdens, needs, and desires to you now. Grant me the confidence I need to keep believing that You will answer me. Give me the faith to persist and not give up. If I have prayed for anything amiss, then please show me. Instruct me and teach me the way I should go. Guide me with Your loving eye, in Jesus' name I pray. Amen."

Faith by works: If you have prayed for something by yourself for a long time, I would like to encourage you to find someone of faith to pray with. There is power in agreement in prayer. Meditate on Jesus' words in Matthew 18:19. I prayed for years for a husband. But it wasn't until I found a believing friend to pray with me (who believed in marriage being the will of God for me) that things started to happen. God loves it when you act on His words and promises. Be blessed today!

Wave Three

Completion of Time

"To everything there is a season, a time for every purpose under Heaven." Eccl.3:1

Back in 2002, as I testified in chapter one, I got born again in the Holy Spirit. I was so fulfilled and happy in Jesus, that I had no desire to marry in life. The Lord had told me on several occasions not to have any male friends. It was a time of holiness, healing, and growth for me. It lasted for years. When I came off the Mission field I went into a time of transition. Flowing in the seasons God has for us is not always easy. We need a change of mind or a change of heart. God was changing my heart and started to talk to me about getting married. By this time, I had been single for so long, the thought of marriage scared me. But as years went on, I started to pray intensely and longed to be with a like-minded man of faith. You see God is the one who puts desires in our hearts. Way too often we sabotage ourselves out of those desires, thinking we need to sacrifice. I struggled for years with the thought of serving Jesus, versus serving a husband. But God started to make it very clear that He wanted marriage for me. Well, I was not getting younger, and it felt like a long hard wait. Often doubting myself and doubting God's will. But then one Summer I went to a Charismatic Christian conference. A well-known Dutch Pastor was speaking. I had heard him preach and prophesy many times before. This time however he was sharing a story I never heard him share before. He said when he was eighteen years old the Lord showed him that he was to bear a Cross. And that cross was to stay single. And then he saw a vision of the future. He saw that when he was forty years old, the cross was taken away, and he would get married. God was speaking to me through that story. He showed me that my time for marriage was at hand. The Autumn following that Summer, I made a trip to the USA to attend a wedding and see some friends. Again, God started speaking to me about a husband, and that the man I would marry was living in the USA. I met up with a friend a few days later in Dallas and she had brought a little blue cloth. As she was praying for me to see me, she felt the Lord bring the little old rhyme to her mind; "Something old, something new, something borrowed, something blue.." That was another prophetic sign! You see when God His time is complete, He will increase the signs and senses in the Spirit. That is if you are paying attention! From there on, everything started to accelerate. I started to pray with a trusted friend, agreeing in prayer for God to bring the man that He had chosen for me. I prayed with her a few times a week as I felt the time was drawing close. I didn't want to make mistakes! Then I met a man three weeks later. He made me laugh. He touched my heart. He loved Jesus and had a childlike faith like me. We video-called for about two weeks. I was still uncomfortable in some ways, but the Holy Spirit was flowing so powerfully between us, I could not stop God! One morning at two a.m. the Lord woke me up and said, "He is going to ask you to marry him, what will be your answer?" How about that for a word from the Lord? Ha ha! When I checked my emails that morning, Chris had written me an email asking if I wanted to marry him. He wrote that he would ask me in person as well. It was a very exciting time as you can imagine. We married nine months later in the USA, a month after I had turned forty. The Angels of God were rejoicing all around us. A time that God had ordained was now completed. It wasn't easy to wait, but God had planned it that way for His reasons. *"For as the heavens are higher than the earth, so are My ways higher than your ways, and My thoughts than your thoughts." Isaiah 55:9.* God is a loving Father. He knows us better than we do ourselves. We can trust Him during the wait. My marriage has been great, wonderful, and fruitful. Praise the Lord!

God His timing and our timing are dissimilar. They don't match unless we completely surrender ourselves to Him. We live in a world of clocks, schedules, agendas, goals, and deadlines. God in His grace will meet us there. But in the days of Abraham, when none of those clocks existed, the beloved Patriarch still had to wait on God for the promised son. When we wait on God to answer our deepest desires, we are challenged with doubts, fears, and unbelief. This is where the core of our faith and heart for God gets tested. However, we have a great Comforter that was given to us to strengthen us in our faith; The precious

Holy Spirit! Paul gave us a great statement about being led by the Spirit. He writes, *"For as many as are led by the Spirit of God, these are sons of God." Romans 8:14.* This is where we see the distinction. The Bible gives us a clear example of King Saul, versus King David. Saul could not wait for God and took the matter into his own hands. David learned to wait on God. It took many years to see his Kingdom anointing come to pass. He had to live like a fugitive, being taunted and ridiculed. All because his heart was to serve the living God. Out of his distress came forth beautiful comforting words; *"Wait on the LORD; be of good courage, and He shall strengthen your heart; wait, I say, on the LORD!" Psalm 27:14*

Ten is the number of testimony. One has to do a little Hebrew thinking here. The Ten Commandments are the Testimony of God; His covenant, as stated in Exodus 31:18, *"He gave Moses two tablets of the Testimony, tablets of stone, written with the finger of God."* And in Deuteronomy 4:13, *"So He declared to you His covenant which He commanded you to perform, the Ten Commandments; and He wrote them on two tablets of stone."* The number ten in Hebrew is the letter yod. Which, from ancient picture language, means; arm or hand. Remember how the Finger of God wrote the Ten Commandments? Jesus, who fulfilled the Law and the Prophets, wrote on the ground with His finger, at the stones of the Temple court. The religious people of the day wanted to condemn the adulterous woman, but He in His Divine wisdom answered them to throw the first stone if they had not sinned. The testimony of God always speaks. And it helps when we know His heart and His ways. When we understand the ways of God and how He thinks and operates, we can better flow in the Spirit and live the Divine life we have in Christ Jesus!

Prayer time: "Almighty God, You hold my times in Your hands. Thank you for being with me all the days of my life. Your plans for me are a future and a hope. I commit myself anew to You and surrender my timing to you. Help me to trust You that your timing is perfect. Help me to understand the season I am in right now, so I can walk in peace and receive Your love and grace. In Jesus' name, I pray. Amen."

Faith by works: Do you have any buried dreams or desires? You probably buried them because they didn't happen when you wanted them to happen. Would you be willing to bring them to the Lord, asking Him about them? Here are some words from King David to encourage you. *"Trust in the LORD, and do good. Dwell in the land, and feed on His faithfulness. Delight yourself also in the LORD, and He shall give you the desires of your heart. Commit your way to the LORD, trust also in Him, and He shall bring it to pass." Psalm 37:3-5*

Wave Four

Divine Healing

"For I am the LORD who heals you." Exodus 15:26

One day I woke up with terrible pain in my bowels. Everything I ate went straight through me. It wasn't the stomach flu as you may think. For days I could not hold any food and everything inside of me was hurting. I lost weight quickly and felt very weak. I knew the Lord had shown me a few months before that I should change my diet. But I had fallen back into old habits. I simply consumed too much fat and dairy. But now I could not hold any food inside. After being knocked out for several days I asked the Lord what the problem was. I heard in my Spirit the following words; "overactive gallbladder." I asked the Lord what I could do about it and He said very clearly, "Speak to it!" So, I spoke to my gallbladder. I didn't find the words for it in the Bible, but I believe that the Holy Spirit in me has the authority to set things straight. I had learned that years before when I was suffering from hormonal imbalance issues. I learned to speak to my own body bringing everything under the authority and submission of Christ. And so I did with my gallbladder, and it calmed down! I immediately felt it in my body! The days after that I only ate cooked vegetables and rice. A few weeks later, I could eat bread and grains again. I have continued to keep a low-fat diet, but God completely restored my health!

It has always been God's heart to heal us and make us whole. We know from the prophet Isaiah's words that Christ took on Himself all our sins and iniquity. And by His stripes, we are healed. David writes in Psalm 103, *"Bless the LORD, O my soul, and forget not His benefits; who forgives all your iniquities, who heals all your diseases..."* So whether we like it or not, sickness seems to be related to sin and iniquity. There are numerous examples in the Bible where the people of God faced plaques or leprosy because of sin. This is a big topic and I am no Theologian. All I know is when Jesus came and they brought the sick, lame, and blind to Him *"He healed them all." Matthew 12:15.* In Jesus we can be healed from any sickness or ailment. We will have what we believe. If we don't believe in Divine healing, we deprive ourselves of the riches and glory in Christ Jesus. One time I was having pains in my chest near my heart and it kept coming back. I have a habit of asking the Lord pretty much everything that I don't understand. So, I asked Him about it saying, "Lord, what is this pain? Is this my heart or my stomach? And He said, "None of it!" So I took it as something the enemy tried to put on me. I pretty much ignored it and it went away! I am not saying we can't have physical pain or illness. When I run too fast and do not take time to rest, I feel it in my body. I have many weaknesses. But I had to let my Medical mindset of pathology go because it is a belief system as well. I worked in a Hospital Lab for several years and often saw scientifically unexplainable things. Some people died of a certain illness and others lived. We have been programmed to be afraid of disease, but the word of God says that we have not been given a spirit of fear, but of love, power, and a sound mind. Have you noticed, when you are anxious or fearful you tend to lose your sound mind? At least I do. I can't seem to discern or think straight when I walk in fear.

And fear wreaks havoc on our soul, which affects our body as well.

You can take Divine healing to any level you want because the word of God never fails. And man walks by what he believes. In my experience, three Divine streams lead to healing. There is the heart. I call it the receiver of God's love. It is our end of the "Divine phone line" to which God speaks. Forgiving those who trespassed against us, was built in the Lord's prayer to us. People suffer all kinds of ailments because they are holding onto unforgiveness, bitterness, and resentment. I had a good relationship with both my parents. However, when I started to forgive them from my heart for their mistakes, I experienced healing in my body from aching joints.

The second Divine stream of Healing flows through the Holy Spirit's gifts of Healing and miracles. That gift, like any other gift of the Holy Spirit, was given to the body of Christ, the Church, as Paul states in 1 Corinthians 12. I happen to know a couple of people who walk in the Holy Spirit's gifts of Healing and miracles. One of them, her name is Aliss Cresswell, a Minister from the UK. I owe much to her because God has given me great friends through their Ministry called Spirit Lifestyle. And

I have been leading groups using their Teaching materials. Aliss has a Divine combination of compassion for people and releasing Jesus His healing over them. I have seen her heal people from MS, Fibromyalgia, eye problems, broken bones, and many other ailments. *"Jesus Christ is the same yesterday, today, and forever!" Hebrews 13:8*

The third Divine stream leading to healing is the Word of God, who is also Jesus! We can read of this beautiful manifestation of Divinity in the first chapter of John's Gospel. *"In the beginning was the Word, and the Word was with God, and the Word was God."* To understand how God's Word heals, I will have to take you into the Hebrew mindset a little. In the Hebrew language, the word for Word is *davar*, which has multiple meanings. It also means to 'talk', a 'thing', or 'substance'. Jewish people will hardly ever read the Bible silently. They talk it, they speak it out loud. Words spoken create substance. The Hebrew letters have numerical value as well. The letter *mem* is the number 40. Place the mem before the word davar, and you get the word 'speaking'; *medaber*. That word, can also be pronounced differently; 'Midbar.' meaning desert in Hebrew. The book of Numbers is called Bamidbar in Hebrew, which means 'In the desert'. But as you have learned now, the word desert has 'the Word' in it. "Now the LORD spoke to Moses in the desert of Sinai." Numbers 1:1. God spoke for forty years *medaber.* His words to His people in the desert. He created a new Nation by His words. He healed them from slavery and reproach. If they kept His Words, they would have no diseases. It was in that context that He said, *"For I am the LORD who heals you." Exodus 15:26.*

The writer of Hebrews says, *"The word of God is living and powerful, and sharper than any two-edged sword, piercing even to the division of soul and spirit, and of joints and marrow, and is a discerner of the thoughts and intents of the heart." Hebrews 4:12*

Another example of healing by the Word of God is fertility. From age fourteen till age thirty I never had any regular female cycle. Sometimes it stayed away for months without any real reason. I never really worried about it because I wasn't married. As I was new to the Charismatic Church, I asked a lady if she thought God could heal my menstruation cycle. She, full of faith, said, "Of course!" And she prayed with me. When I came home, I sat outside in the grass eating my lunch. Two white butterflies came flying towards me, they flew a circle around me, and then together they left. I knew that was my sign from Heaven. From that time on I had a normal monthly female cycle. God had answered our prayer. It was a true miracle! Now fast forward. I didn't get married until I was forty years old. But I became pregnant in the second month of our marriage. Great joy at first, but unfortunately, we lost that baby in the eleventh week of pregnancy. As you understand it was a very traumatic experience. If you have been through the same, I want to give you a big hug right now. Know that no child is lost in Heaven and you will see your son or daughter again one day in the glory of God! The weeks after that terrible miscarriage, the Lord comforted me with the promise of a son. He had told me ten years before my marriage that I would have a son one day and call him "Joshua." It was a secret I had kept in my heart for years. The Lord was simply reminding me of His promise to me. I wasn't hopeless, but any woman knows that waiting to get pregnant is just emotionally draining. The Holy Spirit led me to a very powerful promise in the Bible that I kept in front of my eyes. *"No one shall suffer miscarriage or be barren in your land; I will fulfill the number of your days." Exodus 23:26.* I stood on God's promise each day and spoke it out to keep my faith alive. When I conceived again two years later, I was warring in my Spirit with the Word of God to keep this child. I prayed Bible verses over him every day. He was a healthy boy in the womb and I had a great pregnancy, praise God! Our son was born in June 2015. My husband said he had gold glitter on his head. God is faithful and kept His promise to me. *"God is not a man, that He should lie." Numbers 23:19.* After many years of struggles Job concluded with these wonderful words; *"I know that You can do everything and that no purpose of Yours can be withheld from You."*

When we have faith in God His word and promises, we can also agree with others regarding their prayer needs. One day I wrote the Bible verse that God gave me on a notecard and gave it to a lady in Church. She had been married for years but was still barren. I prayed with her and not long after that she became pregnant and delivered a healthy boy nine months later. When we moved to the neighborhood where we live now, one of my neighbors asked me to come for lunch one day. Her daughter at that time was four years old. She told me how she had suffered about five miscarriages over the past years. Tears were rolling down her face and I could feel her pain. I asked her if she had a Bible laying around and she brought me her Spanish Bible. I showed her the Scripture in Exodus 23:26 and prayed for her. Not long after that, she became pregnant! Nine months later she delivered a healthy baby girl. And she even had more children after that. God will keep His promised Word!

I have many more testimonies of God's healing that will not fit in this book. He healed me of a knee injury, a broken heart, and childhood traumas. Nothing is too small or too big for Him! I hope and pray that you will find the strength to believe that God wants to heal you and restore your life.

Prayer time: "Dear Lord, thank You for all the promises You made to us Your children. And that You are willing and able to heal me. I pray that You help me believe You, so that I can receive healing in my body and soul right now, In Jesus' name. Amen."

Faith by works: Do you have any ailments or battle a disease? Why not ask the Lord what the true cause of it is? He is always willing to reveal the truth of the matter, so we can pull it up by the root and not just combat symptoms. The writer of Hebrews helps us to see how we can be healed as well, showing us to make straight paths, pursue peace and let go of any bitterness. Please read it for yourself in Hebrews 12:12-15.

Wave Five

Prophetic Intercession

"Therefore, He is also able to save to the uttermost those who come to God through Him, since He always lives to make intercession for them. Hebrews 7:25

When the whole world condemns a sinner for his deeds, the Lord is looking on the earth to find someone to stand in the gap. When I lived in Holland, I had a neighbor once, who was kind of a mystery. I can't say this for sure but most likely he had fled his home country for obscure reasons. He spoke no Dutch, or English. He was in his late sixties and walked with a cane. I had befriended him because he had no family. He wasn't very active and would ask me for help at times. He seemed to suffer from several health issues. At times he thought he had heart problems and would fall into a panic. The ambulance had come for him a few times, but they never took him to the Hospital. One evening, he called me again. I went downstairs to see him and he insisted I call the Ambulance. While we were waiting for the medics to come, I asked him if I could pray. But because of the huge language barrier, there was not much understanding. I then asked him in simple words if he believed in Jesus. And he nodded. When the medics came, I went back upstairs to my apartment. As soon as I got inside, I fell into such fierce intercession for him, I paced up and down my apartment. There was a war going on over his soul and the Lord let me fight it, standing in the gap. Asking God for forgiveness for this man's sins. I even commanded the devil to leave as he came for the man's soul. It was unlike any intercession I had done before. After an hour or so the burden lifted and I went to bed. When I came home the next day, two nurses were peeking through his window. I told them that he usually left a key on the window seal. They said it wasn't there. They could see him lying on his bed. When they finally got into his apartment, they found out that he had died. I understood then why the Lord wanted me to intercede so fiercely over his soul. I believe he went to see Jesus. When we packed up his apartment, I found a little orthodox Christian picture of Jesus. It made me cry. Later we found out from his intake records that he had a wife and a son in his native country. It was a sad ending to this man's life. But praise God for Jesus's saving grace!

Engaging in prophetic intercession is like being a lion and a lamb. The lamb lays down itself to intercede for others. The lion rises to action to conquer territory for the King. We read in the Prophetic books of the Bible how Daniel, Ezekiel, and Jeremiah, all carried heavy burdens to pray and prophesy. The calling on us as Christians to be a Royal Priesthood is twofold. To intercede means to stand in the gap for God's people. And to be a Priest, one also speaks on behalf of God to the people. That is what we do when we share the Gospel of Christ Jesus.

There are so many ways to pray and commune with the Father in Heaven. However, I believe intercession can only flow by the Holy Spirit's power through us. I consider it a calling and not so much a choice. Sometimes it literally "falls" on me. I remember a few years ago I was home and the burden for a (notorious) politician fell on me. I wept over that woman on my knees for a good while. I was crying out to God to open her eyes and forgive her for her sins. For that reason, I rather not speak evil about anyone, because in God's eyes, someone can still turn back to Him. I can't just pray with love for someone and then turn my heart to hate them. I hate their evil deeds, but God's words still speak when He said, *"I have no pleasure in the death of the wicked, but that the wicked turn from his way and live."* *Ezekiel 33:11*

I worked for a Ministry that was based in the Old City of Jerusalem, called CMJ. When I didn't have early morning duties, I would go out sometimes, and walk up the Mount of Olives to pray. I used to carry a sheet of paper, a written prayer from a father in the faith; Derek Prince. The prayers were for Jerusalem and Israel, taken from the Word of God. Well, one day as I walked up, a man jumped towards me carrying a knife and pointing it at my body. Since it was so early in the morning, there were no other people around. I had heard stories of tourists being killed. But immediately I felt an Angelic presence covering me and great peace surrounded me. A voice of an Angel said to me, "That won't kill you!" So, I stayed calm. The man demand-ed I give him money, but he started to act very distressed and fearful. I told him I had none, which was true. He kept repeating that he wanted money, threatening me with his knife. To ease his mind, I handed over my purse. It only held the prayer sheet, a bottle of water, and my old Dutch Bible. He ran off. He must have felt terrible! The enemy will try to intimidate you when you make a stand for God. But know that our lives are in His hands.

Do you know that there are two spiritual cities? Jerusalem and Babylon. One is for the Bride of Christ, the other is where the mother of Harlots lives. Jerusalem, also called the third Heaven is mostly known among Christians. But there is also a "second" heaven, a wicked Kingdom, where dark forces rule and demons occupy the souls of men. That is Babylon. The Bible refers to this place several times. You can read it in Isaiah 14 or Jeremiah 50. On those accounts in the Bible, Babylon had been so manifested on earth that God judged and destroyed it. In the eighteenth chapter of the book of Revelation we can read of God's final judgment on this wicked city called Babylon. John describes very vividly what it entails. Satan, dark princes, and demons are spiritually fallen beings. They like to rule over people, cities, and possibly Nations. Most people can't see them because God has not given them for everyone to see. But they are the forces that work against any Christian who walks by the Holy Spirit. They also work overtime to steal, kill and destroy anyone who doesn't walk with Jesus. The good news is that we have been given the authority in Christ over all the power of the enemy. I will explain more about that in the next chapter. Jesus will come back for a Bride that can reign with Him. Reigning with Christ means subduing dark forces that don't comply with the Kingdom of God. This is the initial calling of the Church, the body of Christ. This is what Jesus meant when He said to Peter, *"the gates of hell shall not prevail against it. And I will give you the keys of the Kingdom of Heaven, and whatever you bind on earth will be bound in heaven, and whatever you loose on earth will be loosed in heaven." Matthew 16:18-19.*

Our Gospel preaching efforts will be of little effect until we have dealt with the spiritual dark forces occupying the land, keeping people's souls' captive. We need to go to war with the Word of God to subdue our enemies and set the captives free! Hebrews 11 gives an account of God's people, *"who through faith subdued kingdoms, worked righteousness, obtained promises, stopped the mouths of lions."* I hope that stirs up your spirit. Do you feel the warrior inside of you? Rise up my friend and get yourselves enlisted in God's Army, we have the battle to fight on this earth! *"The LORD said to my Lord, "Sit at My right hand, till I make your enemies Your footstool." The LORD shall send the rod of Your strength out of Zion. Rule in the midst of Your enemies! Your people shall be volunteers in the day of Your power;" Psalm 110:1-3.*

When we lived in Texas, I was praying one day for the Town we lived in. Then in my Spirit, I saw a dark prince parading himself on one of the main streets. He was dressed in a robe, yet the robe and the being had no color and no light. An absolute dark prince. The prince however was acting as if he owned the Town. I was pretty stunned. I knew God was allowing me to see this because He wanted us to dethrone this principality. We did some research and found out why the enemy had been given access to the Town. We went into prayer with the group and took action on what God had revealed to us. *"Now thanks be to God who always leads us in triumph in Christ, and through us diffuses the fragrance of His knowledge in every place." 2 Cor.2:14*

Paul, in Ephesians six, describes how we wrestle against principalities, powers, rulers of darkness, and hosts of wickedness in the heavenly places. He then gives a wonderful description of the Armor God gave us in Christ to withstand and overcome. Christ gave us authority over all the power of the enemy. Let's pray!

Prayer time: "Dear Lord, thank You for all that You do for us. I want to be more like You and have a heart for the lost and the captives. I ask You that You give me Your heart and intercession for what moves You. That I can see and pray for what needs to be accomplished here on earth. Help me to not be fainthearted when the enemy tries to intimidate me but to know that nothing can separate me from Your love in Christ Jesus. Amen.

Faith by works: Find someone that shares a burden for your Town or City and start praying together!

Wave Six

Authority in Christ

"Behold, I give you authority to trample on serpents and scorpions, and over all the power of the enemy, and nothing shall by any means hurt you." Luke 10:19

I believe we all have a built in warrior mentality. It just needs to be awakened in us by the Holy Spirit. I was a defeated Christian for nearly thirty years. But when I learned about the authority we have in Christ, the whole game changed! It started when I entered a powerful Spirit-filled Church. Someone was testifying about how he cast out a demon from his neighbor's house. A spirit that was there causing trouble and terror. This was not long after I got born again. After I heard that testimony, my heart started beating faster and I felt an inner battle. I remember walking up to the front rows where the Pastor and leaders were seated. As I walked down, something like an invisible force grabbed my throat. The next thing I know is that I am in the front row, I fall to the ground and some invisible force inside of me manifests in ways I could not control. The Pastor, his wife, and a few others all started praying and commanded the demon to come out of me. After a minute or so it felt as if a Spiritual "hammer" hit my head. The power of God came over me and I saw a dark shadowy witch spirit leave my body. I never screamed, but now I yelled at it, "leave me, get out of me." As it completely left my body I was like "one dead", like the boy in Mark nine. All my muscles, nerves, and cells seem to relax. The Church leaders had to pick me up. They sat me on a chair and prayed over me some more. I had never seen anyone being delivered from a demon in my life, but I knew that was what happened to me. I felt so light and free! HalleluYah for the authority we have in Christ Jesus! After that, the Holy Spirit led me into a fast. It was a minor version of what happened to Jesus in the wilderness. I was now facing the spiritual forces that had kept me back from my destiny in God for thirty years. I was working in a

Christian Bookstore at the time, and a girl that worked there recommended a book to me. It was called, "And they shall expel demons" by Derek Prince. During my fast, I read his book, and my eyes were opened! I learned how demons enter your life through doctrines, lies, new-age practices, and sin. After every few pages, I would fall into warfare with some sort of demon that would manifest itself. I was now learning to take my authority in Christ to overcome these demonic forces. It was boot camp with Jesus in the wilderness. I didn't eat for two weeks. But I had now faced the demons and overcame them in Christ Jesus!

The next move of discipleship came when the Lord led me to join a City-wide prayer group. I learned there that people are bound in the spirit by principalities and powers that rule over cities. I learned about idolatry and witchcraft and how to battle those forces in prayer together. I write about these things because the Lord wants His people to know that they have the authority in Christ to pull down the strongholds. Setting the captives free! Not long after I learned to take authority over the enemy's power in cities, the Lord sent me to Jerusalem in Israel. He had given me a Scripture that I had to hold on to for years. *"No one engaged in warfare entangles himself with the affairs of this life, that he may please him who enlisted him as a soldier."* *2 Timothy 2:4.* I had become a watchman on the walls of Jerusalem. A city in continuous warfare. Did you know as we speak the Word of the Lord, that Angels hearken to it and fight on our behalf? I will describe more about the ministering Angels of God in wave number nine. I do not want to make you believe that it was by my power I did those things. I simply learned to operate in the Christ-given authority that every believer has.

The Bible refers several times to God's children as an Army. The children of Israel that came out of Egypt transitioned from slaves to freedom. Yet they had to be trained to fight, as they were now facing enemies trying to keep them from entering the Promised Land. Another account of awakening can be found in Ezekiel chapter thirty-seven. After years of exile in Babylon, again the Lord was speaking about His children as a raised-up Army. They went from being spiritually dead and scattered, to being Spiritually alive and gathered together! *"The LORD gives voice before His army, for His camp is very great; For strong is the One who executes His word." Joel 2:11*

God wants His people to inherit the earth. We have an enemy that tries to take over this earth. Jesus needs His Army and therefore He has given us the authority over all the power of the enemy. We will enter another era of the Medieval Dark Ages if God's people do not rise to their God-given authority to trample the serpents and scorpions! There are souls to be saved and Nations to be conquered for Christ.

We can preach the Gospel, but if people are bound by spiritual lies and principalities that rule over cities, there will not be much fruit of our labor. *"The weapons of our warfare are not carnal, but mighty in God for pulling down strongholds" 2 Cor.10:4*

Back when I lived in my hometown, I cycled a lot. It would take me an hour or so to ride my bicycle around the whole Town. As I rode through the agricultural fields, I would often pray for the Town and its people. One day I came back into Town and saw they had hung up advertisements for a show with a spiritist, also called a psychic. Immediately, something arose inside of me saying, "Not in my Town!" I prayed and took authority in the Spirit over any "intruders" trying to come in. These spiritists bind ignorant people to demonic entities by deception and flattering tongues. Not long before the date of the show, I heard it had been canceled.

Just like Jesus' disciples, when we are new to this revelation of authority in Christ, we need to grow in faith, strength, and authority. Wisdom needs to be applied when we go into battle. I have made many mistakes and learned from them. Demons and dark forces find 'rights' to be somewhere if someone opens the door. We need to repent, renounce, break dark covenants, and do away with sin before we can completely close the doors to darkness. More on this subject you can find in the Appendix of this book.

Prayer time: "Lord of the Heavenly Armies, I thank You for always fighting on our behalf. I ask You to open the eyes of my understanding to know the authority I have in You. Help me Lord to be brave and courageous. To take my place in Your Army as a good soldier of Jesus Christ. In His name, I pray. Amen.

Faith by works: Ask God to show you if any powers of darkness are operating in your life. Then wait till the Holy Spirit will shine His light on them. In the Appendix, you can find the steps to get free from darkness and demons.

Wave Seven

The Gifts of the Holy Spirit

"There are diversities of gifts, but the same Spirit."
1 Corinthians 12:4

I have taught several classes on how to walk in the Spiritual gifts. When people start to be more aware of how God works, they can flow with it easier, going with the wind of the Holy Spirit. Different personalities operate in different spiritual manifestations. I love all of the manifestations and believe they are always available in God when we ask Him. Paul told the Church in Corinthians, to *"earnestly desire the best gifts."* I was not raised around Pentecostal or Charismatic people, but this is how God met me in my desire to preach the Gospel. One time, I was at a Dutch revival Meeting. I asked this couple to pray for me because I wanted to be an Evangelist. As soon as they prayed for me, the power of God fell on me and I could not stand on my feet anymore. I lay on the floor for a while and when I sat back up, I heard myself speaking in tongues! I had not even asked God for that manifestation, but there it was. Bam! Baptized in the fire.

The next day I prayed for a lady who was suffering all kinds of things. I remember the Holy Spirit's power arose inside of me and spoke with authority. It was about cutting her loose from the power of the enemy. I made a move with my hand as if I had a sword and I cut through something under her feet. Instantly she dropped down on the floor like a puppet whose strings had been cut. Jesus had set her free, and I was amazed. You see, it wasn't "my gift" or my operation, I just spoke words by the Holy Spirit. Words that I had not spoken before, and God's manifest power did the rest in that woman's life. HalleluYah! This is possible because of the finished work of Christ Jesus, our Lord, and Redeemer! This is why the Holy Spirit was given to us. Not just to believe in Christ and be saved, but to walk with power and authority, as Christ did. He trained His disciples to do what He did. His disciples trained others and started communities of believers who walked in the manifested power of the Holy Spirit. Jesus spoke beautiful words about this, *"Most assuredly, I say to you, he who believes in Me, the works that I do he will do also; and greater works than these he will do because I go to My Father." And whatever you ask in My name, that I will do, that the Father may be glorified in the Son. If you ask anything in My name, I will do it." John 14:12-14*

To sum up the gifts of the Holy Spirit in one sentence, I would say they are the power of God revealed to the people of God. You don't need to be Pentecostal to believe or even operate in these gifts. God does not make distinctions between denominations. The first recorded outpouring of the Holy Spirit in the USA happened to be on Baptists and Presbyterians! And it happened not far from where I live; in Murphy, North Carolina. But let's look at the original text from Paul's letter. Because I find that the English translation of these Divine power manifestations does not do justice. If we look at the Holy Spirit's manifestations as gifts that God hands out, then we can believe He probably skipped us. It is not something we own, possess, or walk in by our own doing. The Greek word here is, "khar-is-mah", meaning a Divine gratuity or spiritual endowment. God, by His Holy Spirit, can manifest His power in any way or form needed when He sees people that can receive it. He works through imperfect people and receives all the glory as He should. When I minister to people, I am simply "borrowing" His power to get someone free, healed, or delivered from the enemy. Other people call it "operating in the gifts." We can train our spiritual senses to walk out our Christian Ministry in these grace-given Divine powers.

I will share with you another way how the Holy Spirit gifts can operate. This has happened to me a few times now. I would pray for someone and then the Spirit shows me a place where they would move to. I had it for a friend in Texas. It usually doesn't make sense at that very time, but when time is completed in God, everything falls into place and the move makes sense. Those friends in Texas did move to the place where the Lord showed me. Another example of prophetic words that didn't make sense at first is the following. I was praying over the phone with a friend that lived close by. She then asked me if I heard any words from the Lord for her. I remained silent to listen to the Holy Spirit, and I heard the word, "Moving!" A few months before that, I had seen in the Spirit they would move houses in a northern direction. These were clear words I heard the Spirit say. Anyways, my friend thanked me for the word. But it made no sense because they were about to build their own home! They were already living on their property for three years but hadn't built their house yet. Ten months later, however, when their house had been built and they had moved in, the Lord dropped it on them to sell the house and move! They sold their newly built house for a great price and moved up north! I had nothing to do with it. God said it, not me. Prophetic words are powerful. They are God's signposts to direct us where He wants us to go.

Faith is another beautiful manifestation the Holy Spirit gives us. God gave me faith to go to Israel and from there on He led me to the Ministry that He wanted me to work for. I went by faith, like Abraham not knowing where I was going to end up. I had no contact or address. But as I walked around Jerusalem one day the Holy Spirit led me to go to a Christian compound that had a restaurant, guesthouse, and a chapel. I told the people how the Lord told me to go to Jerusalem, not knowing what I should do there. They told me they needed help, so I stayed and worked in the guesthouse with them. It's okay not to have everything planned out in life. *"For we walk by faith, not by sight." 2 Cor.5:7.* God promises you the following: *"I will instruct you and teach you in the way you should go; I will guide you with My eye." Psalm 32:8.* When we walk in the power of the Holy Spirit, we can rest assured we are walking out our destiny in God.

Back to the Holy Spirit manifestations. Paul wrote all about these in his first letter to the Corinthians. Chapter twelve lists the Holy Spirit's gifts of; wisdom, knowledge, faith, healing, miracles, prophesy, discernment of spirits, tongues, and interpretation of tongues. Jesus walked in the power of the Holy Spirit, and *"he who is joined to the Lord is one spirit with Him." 1 Cor. 6:17.* I have seen every one of those beautiful gifts in action and the fruits of it. The Holy Spirit builds up, heals, delivers, strengthens, and comforts the body of Christ. A lot of Christians get afraid and religiously offended when they hear someone prophesy or release revelation knowledge from God. Why? What are they afraid of? Just watch and see what fruit it produces and test the spirits, as John told us. I grew up with a distant God image, but when I had my encounter with the presence and power of God, He became close and intimate. And that is the God I still serve today. *"He is the Beginning and the End, says the Lord, "who is and who was and who is to come, the Almighty." Rev.1:8.* He is close and near when someone receives a very specific word of knowledge. It goes right into the heart of the person as they feel God acknowledges them and cares. It's a beautiful Ministry, very precious and glorious.

Prayer time: "Father God, You are the One true God. Thank You for giving us the Holy Spirit. I ask You that You help me to walk in the gifts of the Holy Spirit. You made them available to us to build up the Church. I ask You that You give me faith and boldness to step out in the gifts of the Holy Spirit, in Jesus' name I pray. Amen."

Faith by works: If you are ready to be consumed by the presence of God, then you can ask Him to baptize you with fire. He will lead you to a place where someone can lay hands on you and set you on fire for Jesus. Be prepared to pray in tongues and feel the power of God!

Wave Eight

Visions

"And it shall come to pass afterward that I will pour out My Spirit on all flesh; your sons and your daughters shall prophesy, your old men shall dream dreams, your young men shall see visions." Joel 2:28

When I was between six and eight years old, I started to have visions. One vision was repeated to me several times when I was a child. It came to me like an open vision. This means you see things with your spirit eyes, while you are fully awake. I was sitting in our living room looking outside at the clouded sky. Then I saw stars or planets appear close to me as if the sky between heaven and earth was gone. At the end I would see a big red planet, perhaps it was an eclipsed moon. After that, I would see chaos on the earth and planes crashing. I would see smoke rising. I never had a sense of fear when I saw the vision. I simply didn't know what it meant. But my Spirit seemed to know because I felt a great sense of purpose for myself. I knew I had to save people in that time of trouble. I never shared these visions with my parents, but one time, when I was sleeping, I woke up from a very bright light in my bedroom. I opened the bedroom curtain and saw another amazing vision. I saw Jesus coming back on the clouds of Heaven! O HalleluYah, what a glorious day that will be for those who are His! I was so excited that I ran to my parent's bedroom. I woke my mother, saying, "Jesus is here, He is coming back!" My mother thought I had been dreaming and put me back in bed.

A vision can come in a picture or a scene play, but you see it with the eyes of your spirit. Sometimes you can have a vision and be in it yourself. It is a different world; it is the Spirit world. My son once told me that before he fell asleep, he saw a movie. God gave him a vision in which he saw the Army Angels of Heaven in full action! As God's sons and daughters, born by the Holy Spirit we can all see in the Spirit. It seems to be a 'lost' trade for most Western world Christians. For the past decade, I have helped people to hear the voice of God, desire the Gifts of the Holy Spirit, and to step out in faith. Why? Because Jesus told us that signs and wonders would follow those who believe. His Kingdom is not of this world. To make disciples effectively and walk in the authority of Christ, we need our Spiritual senses to be activated.

Years later, when I was living in Jerusalem, the Lord brought those childhood visions back to my memory. He did this in a very profound way. I walked out of the Old City one day. Right before I came to the City gate, I saw all these figs laying on the ground. A strong wind had been blowing. I looked at them and I heard in my Spirit the Scripture that says, *"And the stars of heaven fell to the earth, as a fig tree drops its late figs when it is shaken by a mighty wind. Then the sky receded as a scroll when it is rolled up,..."* *Revelation 6:13-14.* When I was back home, I started to search the Scriptures. In those years I was surrounded by great Bible teachers and scholars. I had learned that God has foretold everything and that truth would always be witnessed by two or three prophets. Then I found in the book of Joel the following verses, *"And I will show wonders in the heavens and in the earth: blood and fire and pillars of smoke. The sun shall be turned into darkness, and the moon into blood, before the coming of the great and awesome day of the LORD." Joel 2:31*

With that vision, I believe the Lord showed me the opening of the sixth seal, that is about to happen.

Sometimes I see things in the Spirit that are not as prophetic as the one I just described. Many years ago when I was part of a small congregation, I kept seeing a vision of several people holding up shields. A shower of enemy arrows came, but the shields melted into a roof and the arrows were of no effect. Then I saw a man standing by himself. He had a shield as well, but as the arrows came, some were shielded off, but others pierced him. I felt this was a vision for the Church I was part of. However, week after week when I came I didn't feel the Lord's prompting to tell the Pastor. After several weeks, the Holy Spirit urged me to go to the Pastor and share my vision. He then gave me the microphone to share with the congregation. Up till that point, I had no idea why the Lord was showing me what He did. But after I had finished sharing, the Spirit spoke the following words; "This is for you, you may feel you stand alone, but the Lord wants you to know that you belong to this congregation, to this family of believers."

After the service a couple came up to me and the man said, "That was for me!" Apparently, he had felt rejected and judged over some relationship issues and had not come to Church in four weeks, he told me. I was baffled with God's care for that one man. That's our Father's love!

How about you? Have you seen any visions from God? Do you believe God would want you to engage in what He wants to do on the earth? Do you feel called by Him, but do not fully understand your calling? Let's pray with me;

Prayer time: "Lord, thank You for calling me into Your Kingdom. I pray that You will open the eyes of my spirit, so I can see what You see. I ask You to enlighten the eyes of my understanding so that I will know the hope of Your calling. And that I may know the exceeding greatness of Your power towards me, according to the working of Your mighty power in Jesus Christ. In His name, I pray. Amen."

Faith by works: When you wait on the Lord and see a vision, simply speak out to the Lord what you see. You can then ask Him what He is saying or what it means. And make sure you write it down. You can also revisit your visions with the Lord, asking Him again what He is saying. In Jeremiah 1:11-14 you will read how God operates that way for a purpose. Peter, like me as a child, also had a repeated vision. Visions often are strange to our under-standing, but when we pay close attention, we realize that it is God speaking! For Peter, it became the revelatory door to preach the Gospel to the Gentiles. You can read about his experience in Acts 10:9-16. Be encouraged and step out in faith!

Wave Nine

Angels of the Most High

"Bless the LORD, you His angels, who excel in strength, who do His word, heeding the voice of His word." Psalm 103:20

O His precious Angels! They are such wonderful created beings. Maybe God keeps most of us blinded to see them because we would fall on our knees, as John the Revelator did, and try to worship them. But truly they carry God's glory and splendor. As I am writing these chapters, I have already concluded that I am limited by my own words. I attempt to describe the power, the splendor, the depth of our Almighty God, but I fail. I will need to add my prayers to this book. That as you read it, the Holy Spirit will take you to the Divine places I try to describe.

Many years ago, I was in fervent prayer for my family. We were sort of stuck in a situation and wanted to move forwards. One night I woke up to the sound of a little kid's toy going off. I walked over to the toy box in the corner but left the lights off. As soon as I reached my hand toward the area where the toy was, I got electrified by the power of God. My whole body started to shake, I had to lie down on the bed again. I knew there was an Angel in the room, but I had to overcome myself to even ask! When God opened my eyes, I saw a Military Angel covered in bronze-looking armor. He wasn't just wearing armor, it was part of his being. He must have been ten feet tall. His arms looked like beams, his legs trained for powerlifting. When I dared to look at his face, I saw such a fierce-looking face that it frightened me. He stood there, with his arms folded like he was waiting on me. I had to rely on the Holy Spirit for what to do next. Mind you it was in the middle of the night. After asking the Angel his name and where he came from, I asked him why he had come. And he replied, "I am waiting on your command!" I was pretty taken aback. This defied my religious framework. Do we give commands to Angels?

Where is that in the Bible? I had heard a lady talk about it before, but I was still in unbelief. I was almost offended. Now my mind was racing with thoughts, so I asked the Holy Spirit again what to do. The Holy Spirit reminded me of the verse in Isaiah 45:11, where God says, *"And concerning the work of My hands, you command Me."* And another occasion where Jesus talks about God providing Him with more than twelve legions of Angels. (Which He didn't utilize because He wanted the Scriptures to be fulfilled.) Then I thought of how the centurion believed that Jesus gave command by His word to the Angels to heal his servant. (Luke 7). I lay on my bed for a good while saying nothing. I even tried to go back to sleep! But the whole room was so electrified I could not sleep in this Angel's presence. Finally, when I crossed the boundaries of my religion, I said something like, "Army Angel of God, I give you the command now to go and destroy all the hindrances of the enemy standing in the way of God's plan for us. And I quoted some verses, like, *"No weapon formed against us shall prosper."* And *"the weapons of my warfare or not carnal but mighty in God.* And I declare to pull down this stronghold coming against us In Jesus' name!" When I was done, the Angel left! A few weeks later, we were able to move out of the situation that we had been stuck in for five months. It was an absolute breakthrough moment and God was teaching me how He operates.

Almost every person in the Bible that walked by faith had encounters with Angels. Angels of God show up at significant times in the history of God's people. And God hasn't changed today. The Apostle Mark heard Jesus say, *"Whatever things you ask when you pray, believe that you receive them, and you will have them."* Does God leave His throne to answer your prayers? Does Jesus go back and forth over the whole earth to answer prayers? I don't think so. He sends His Angels, His *"ministering spirits sent forth to minister for those who will inherit salvation." Hebrews 1:14* tells us.

There are a lot of great books* written these days about the Ministry of Angels and how we as believers can work with these Holy servants of God. These books are especially helpful for those who lead Meetings and want to let the Holy Spirit lead the service. Angels will show up and minister salvation, revelation, or even healing to people. I have seen Angels yielding swords in Meetings to deliver people from darkness. At other times, Angels take on the appearance of man. This often happens in situations of distress, accidents, or great needs. Many of us can recall stories, where they were helped by someone who was instantly on the spot. And how that person also disappeared all of a sudden. *"Do not forget to entertain strangers, for by so doing some have unwittingly entertained angels."* The writer of Hebrews tells us. So, if Angels are with us every day, we can train our Spiritual senses to see, hear and perceive them. I believe anyone awake in his or her spirit can sense other spirits. Whether it is demons or Angels. This is where a lot of "New Age" practices feed into because much of our Christian world walks in total ignorance. We need the Holy Spirit to breathe the life of God into us, so that our spirit comes to life! And we can see with our spiritual eyes what God sees! So that we can worship Him in Spirit and truth, as Jesus told us.

This is such a controversial subject because Satan doesn't want you to find out who is for you and with you when he wages war on your soul. God gave Angels to watch over you, to send you answers to prayers. To tell you of His plans and directions for you. The enemy hates God's Angels because they can overpower him. Religious spirits want to accuse you of not worshiping Jesus if you happen to talk "too much" about Angels. I have kept myself silent for years, talking about them, because I was walking in the fear of men. But the Lord told me to write these testimonies, so I obey Him. I have seen Angels, and yes demons too. And so can you! We seem to be more perceptive in our spirit when distractions are minimized. That's why I often go for a hike and linger in the woods to pray. Away from home, where no chores, screens, or people need my attention. Me and my God. Angels came to minister to Jesus after He went through the temptations of Satan. One time when I felt so beaten up by several hurtful encounters with someone, I laid on my bed feeling worn out. I asked God to heal me and give me strength. Then I felt the presence of two Angels. I call them "Nursing Angels" because that's what they do. They carry the comfort, grace, healing, and hope from God. I lay there still feeling wrapped in God's love. I felt they were touching my soul and healing my wounds. It was as if I had fallen into a deep sleep, yet I was awake. After ten minutes or so, they left and the bedroom door fell open. I was completely healed and restored in my soul! God sent His Angels to answer my prayers. He leads us beside the still waters and restores our souls. These experiences always make us in awe of God and Jesus. Because it is through the finished work of the Cross that we can now be made whole in Him!

Some of the Angels God created are always with us. Most people call them guardian Angels. Others call them Ministry Angels. I have no Theology on this, but in my experience, they are both. Because I have seen my "Guardian Angels" and know their names. (God named all the Angels and created beings in Heaven. He let Adam name everything on earth.) Not only have the Angels protected me throughout my life, but they also helped me to become who I am in God. Their identity is their assignment to us from God. They will help us fulfill our destiny if we walk in obedience to Christ. Angels are charged with God's presence. They love God so much; it radiates from their whole being. They always get excited and joyful when I start witnessing about Jesus or share testimonies of God's power! We have to become like little children and be silent at times to let the Holy Spirit lead us. When we do that, the Angels will be active around us. When I lead Prayer Meetings or teach classes about the gifts of the Spirit, I sense their presence as well.

Angels come in different tribes, ranks, or orders. The Bible gives us a few names for these different types of Angels. The priestly Angel meeting Abraham was from the order of Melchizedek. We know of the Archangels called; Michael and Gabriel. We read about Heavenly Armies of Angels, called Hosts or Tzevaot in Hebrew. Joshua, son of Nun, met the Commander of these Heavenly Armies on his way to conquer the Promised Land. The Armies of Heaven are pretty amazing to behold. I keep a YouTube channel, and interestingly enough the video in which I talk about seeing the Angel Armies has been watched the most. It's called, "Heaven invading the Earth." In it, I share several Angelic visitations I had over the past ten years. And how God has lifted the veil of what He is about to do on this earth. Perhaps it has already started by the time you are reading this book! Glory to the Most High God and Jesus Christ His Son! Who was and is and is to come!

God's Angels are real. They love it when we speak the Word of truth and yield the sword of the Spirit. They will fight on our behalf when we believe we have victory in Christ. Sometimes when I minister to people in a prayer session, a Messenger Angel comes and I hear him speak words in my spirit. As soon as I start to open my mouth to utter what I hear, the power of God comes to the person I minister to. One word from Heaven can heal a heart or set someone free.

Prayer time: "Lord God Almighty, I thank You for watching over me, covering me with Your feathers. Protecting me with Your Angels. I ask You that You open my Spirit eyes to see the Angels you have set over me. Please help me not to miss any Angelic encounters that You have planned for me, to take me into the Promised Land. In Jesus' name, I pray. Amen."

Faith by works: If you are eager to see and perceive more of the Spirit world, I suggest setting some time apart to fast and pray, as the Holy Spirit leads you. When we focus on Spiritual things, that's when we become more aware and awakened to our spiritual senses.

*Book references: Everyday Angels by Charity Virkler. Angels that Gather by Paul Keith Davis.

Wave Ten

The Beauty of Jesus

"How beautiful upon the mountains are the feet of Him who brings good news, Who proclaims peace, Who brings glad tidings of good things." Isaiah 52:7

When I lived in Jerusalem, I would ride the bus to Latrun sometimes to get out of the hustle and bustle of the city. In Latrun there is an old Monastery with several acres of vineyards and hilly farmland. In those days I didn't have many physical friends, but I had a faithful friend in Jesus. He never failed to walk with me. My life was about intercession, ministry, and witnessing those days. One day I was walking in those fields and from behind a bush, a gazelle jumped on the dirt road. He stood there about three yards away, looking straight at me with his brown eyes. The presence of the Lord overwhelmed me so much, I stood there in a trance. Heaven met me right there. The beauty of Jesus His love for me had overtaken me. I don't know how long I stood there, but at some point, the gazelle jumped up and leaped in the air. *"The voice of my beloved! Behold, He comes leaping upon the mountains, skipping upon the hills. My beloved is like a gazelle..." Song of Solomon 2:8-9* When we walk with Him, the Bible, His Word will become real to us.

Jesus is beautiful! He is magnificent, glorious, and powerful. He is also very personal and tender of heart. He is the One and only Savior of the world; Yeshua haMashiach. How can I describe Him? Words are not enough. Jesus is not of this world. His beauty is a heavenly splendor that makes us worship Him. We can look at pictures, and images people painted of Jesus but it is not enough. He is the Son of the Living God! He was and is and is to come!

The beauty of Jesus is not the beauty of this world. Here is another Jerusalem story that illustrates that. I had heard from a Christian friend that there was this strange young guy who walked around with a big wooden Cross. He said God told him to do it to preach the Gospel. In those days, the Christian community in Israel was very cautious about sharing Jesus with the Jews. They would tell me things like, "You can't tell the Jews the Gospel because they have been hurt by Christians too much, just love them." They even told me to not write His name in the emails I wrote home because they would be spying on me. Most Christians were afraid to be "kicked out" of the country if they would be too outspoken about Jesus. Walking with Jesus equals overcoming the fear of men. So, one day I walked out of the Old City gate, and I saw him! The man that my friend had told me about. He was a young man, with a beard and half-long hair, walking with a real-size Cross on his shoulder. Yes, he looked like Jesus! I stopped him. His name was Joseph and he was born in the USA. We talked for a little while. In my Spirit, I knew he was doing what God told him to do. He asked me to pray for him. What he did was offensive to many. He got ridiculed and persecuted. However, he kept on walking his Cross in all kinds of cities, as a prophetic witness of Christ. How symbolic of our beloved Savior who went through it all!

Talking about Jesus makes me emotional. Because He is so near and dear to me. He was always there and will always be. "My beloved is mine, and I am His." The Shulamite bride wrote. Jesus is passionately in love with you! Can you receive it? He wants to conquer your whole heart, can you let Him in? Perhaps you are in a season where your love has grown lukewarm. Life's busyness and distractions seem to do that. Perhaps you feel disappointed by unanswered prayers. You can come to Jesus and bring all that to Him. You can lay down your burdens, your hurt, your pain, and your disappointments at the foot of the Cross. He can take it all away right now. To get close to Jesus again is to remind ourselves of who He is and what He did for us. *"I am the way, the truth, and the life." John 14:6.* Let's talk to Jesus now.

Prayer time: Lord Jesus, I come to You. I'm sorry I haven't talked with You much lately. Please forgive me. I know You love me and want to spend time with me. Please help me to hear Your voice and know Your heart, so that I am more aware of Your presence and beauty in my life. In Your name, I pray, amen."

Faith by works: When I go for a walk by myself, I always invite Jesus to come to walk with me. I talk to Him and then listen. *"My sheep hear My voice,"* He said. He loves to talk to you and show you things, give you the revelation, understanding, or wisdom you need. You can also ask the Lord what He would like to talk about. You will be surprised by what He will share with you!

Ten Waves of Awe

Are you in awe of Him? Jesus is the Darling of Heaven. The desire of all Nations.

"The Bible says my King is the King of the Jews.

He's the King of Israel, He's the King of Righteousness.

He's the King of the ages, He's the King of Heaven.

He's the King of Glory, He's the King of Kings, and the Lord of Lords.

That's my King! I wonder do you know Him?

My King is a sovereign King, no means of measure can define His limitless love.

He's enduringly strong, He's entirely sincere, He's eternally steadfast.

He's immortally graceful, He's imperially powerful, He's impartially merciful.

Do you know Him?

He's the greatest phenomenon that has ever crossed the horizon of this world.

He is God's Son. He's the sinner's Saviour.

He's the centerpiece of civilization. He's unparalleled, He's unprecedented

He's the loftiest idea in literature. He's the highest personality in philosophy

He's the fundamental doctrine of true theology

He's the only One qualified to be an all-sufficient Savior.

I wonder if you know Him today?

He supplies strength for the weak,

He's available for the tempted and the tried

He sympathizes, and He saves

He strengthens and sustains

He guards, and He guides

He heals the sick. He cleansed the lepers

He forgives sinners. He discharges debtors

He delivers the captive, He defends the feeble

He blesses the young, He serves the unfortunate

He regards the aged, He rewards the diligent

And He beautifies the meek.

I wonder if you know Him?

He's the key to knowledge, He's the wellspring of wisdom

He's the doorway of deliverance, He's the pathway of peace

He's the roadway of righteousness, He's the highway of holiness

He's the gateway of glory.

Do you know Him?

His life is matchless, His goodness is limitless

His mercy is everlasting. His love never changes

His word is enough, His grace is sufficient

His reign is righteous and His yoke is easy and His burden is light.

I wish I could describe Him to you

He's indescribable

He's incomprehensible

He's invincible

He's irresistible

You can't get Him out of your mind, you can't get Him off of your hand

You can't outlive Him and you can't live without Him.

The Pharisees couldn't stand Him, but they found out they couldn't stop Him

Pilate couldn't find any fault in Him

Herod couldn't kill Him

Death couldn't handle Him and the grave couldn't hold Him!

Yeah, That's My King!

Taken from a sermon of Dr. S.M. Lockridge, Reverend Pastor of Calvary Baptist Church in San Diego.

Epilogue

"Beloved, let us love one another, for love is of God; and everyone who loves is born of God and knows God. He who does not love does not know God, for God is love. In this the love of God was manifested toward us, that God has sent His only begotten Son into the world, that we might live through Him." 1 John 7-9

Walking the Divine life in Christ is walking in God's love. *"And though I have the gift of prophecy and understanding all mysteries and all knowledge, and though I have all faith so that I could remove mountains, but not have love, I am nothing,"* Paul stated in 1 Corinthians 13:2

When Governments all over the world started to ban people from gathering, because of a sickness that swept through the earth, I asked the Lord about it. He gave me the following words;

"Love gathers, fear separates."

Surely one could feel the fear in the atmosphere. As I was praying, asking the Lord what was happening, He led me to read chapter eighteen of the book of Revelation. It's about Babylon, the spiritual dark kingdom that tries to rule the earth. In verse 23 it says, *"for by your sorcery all nations were deceived."* The word sorcery is originally a Greek word; Pharmakeia. These Pharmaceutical billion-dollar companies surely like to rule the world. But we are of a different Kingdom, hallelujah! Jesus made this statement twice in His prayer for His disciples, saying, *"They are not of the world, just as I am not of the world." John 17:16.* Walking in the Spirit of God often goes contrary to walking in this world. But let no one rob you of your faith! Whatever the Lord calls you to do, do it! I hear Jesus saying to you, *"In the world, you will have tribulation, but be of good cheer, I have overcome the world." John 16:33*

As Christians, we should come out of trials and tribulations shining brighter than before. Not because we are so good or full of faith. But because of our weakness and fears, we seek Him. My grandmother would share that when the Nazis took over my native country, it became very clear who the true Christians were. Some collaborated with the Nazis. Others betrayed those who helped the Jews.

Whatever we will face in our time and age, know that when we walk in the power of the Holy Spirit, we are over-comers in Christ! Jesus wrote in His letters to the Church-es, the admonishing words, "to him who overcomes..."

"And they overcame him by the blood of the Lamb and by the word of their testimony, and they did not love their lives to the death." Revelation 12:11

To the Jewish Reader

Jesus may have been a Christian concept to you all your life. But did you know that Jesus' genealogy is found in Matthew chapter one? He is a descendant of David and Abraham. He is Jewish and is named the Lion of the Tribe of Judah in Heaven. He is also your Messiah!

Most synagogues have omitted the reading of the 53rd chapter of Isaiah the prophet. Call it "the forbidden chapter" but it described vividly what would happen to the Jewish people in time. Read it for yourself;

"Who has believed our report? And to whom has the arm of the Lord been revealed?

For He shall grow up before Him as a tender plant, And as a root out of dry ground. He has no form or comeliness; And when we see Him, There is no beauty that we should desire Him.

He is despised and rejected by men, A Man of sorrows and acquainted with grief. And we hid, as it were, our faces from Him; He was despised, and we did not esteem Him.

Surely He has borne our griefs And carried our sorrows; Yet we esteemed Him stricken, Smitten by God, and afflicted.

But He was wounded for our transgressions, He was bruised for our iniquities; The chastisement for our peace was upon Him, And by His stripes we are healed.

All we like sheep have gone astray; We have turned, every one, to his own way; And the Lord has laid on Him the iniquity of us all.

He was oppressed and He was afflicted, Yet He opened not His mouth; He was led as a lamb to the slaughter, And as a sheep before its shearers is silent, So He opened not His mouth.

He was taken from prison and from judgment, And who will declare His generation? For He was cut off from the land of the living; For the transgressions of My people He was stricken.

And they made His grave with the wicked-- But with the rich at His death, Because He had done no violence, Nor was any deceit in His mouth.

Yet it pleased the Lord to bruise Him; He has put Him to grief. When You make His soul an offering for sin, He shall see His seed, He shall prolong His days, And the pleasure of the Lord shall prosper in His hand.

He shall see the labor of His soul, and be satisfied. By His knowledge My righteous Servant shall justify many, For He shall bear their iniquities.

Therefore I will divide Him a portion with the great, And He shall divide the spoil with the strong, Because He poured out His soul unto death, And He was numbered with the transgressors, And He bore the sin of many, And made intercession for the transgressors."

Isaiah 53:1-13

You are reading this book for a reason. This is Divine destiny for you, your longing to be closer to God, to feel Him, to hear His voice. God is showing you today that Jesus (Yeshua) is your Messiah. He made the perfect atonement for your sins 2000-plus years ago. He rose from the dead and went back to Heaven till His People are ready for His return. He is waiting for you to come home! Will you call on His name with me today? "Yeshua, I believe you are the Messiah, ben Elohim. Please forgive me for my sins. Open my eyes so I can see You. Open my ears so I can hear

Your voice. And please fill my heart with Your love, so I know You are near. In Yeshua's name, amen.

Appendix A

Authority in Christ - How to Get Free from Demons

Let me give you a disclaimer here first. I am not able to cover every spiritual problem in this Appendix. Wonderful Godly people have written books about this topic. I recommend reading some of the listed books below to build your faith if you are completely new to this. There are three short videos on this topic on my YouTube channel as well for you to listen to.

Symptoms of demon influence or possession.

Feeling oppressed, depressed, mental turmoil, unbelief, hatred, doubt about salvation, self-hatred, self-hurt, self-neglect, addictions, extreme moodiness, uncontrollable anger, and compulsion to sin are all signs something is not right in our spirit man. Paul writes to us, *"May your whole spirit, soul, and body be preserved blameless at the coming of our Lord Jesus Christ."* Life starts in our spirit. The Holy Spirit gives us life. From our spirit, life flows into our soul and our body. Physical manifestations of evil spirits are; pain, sickness, fatigue, mental illness, seizures, and stagnation. I have seen so many deliverances and it always strikes me how people felt they could not progress in life. But Jesus came to set the captives free, hallelujah! The enemy has access to our spirit through; sin, lies, and abuse. If you have practiced any forms of idolatry, witchcraft, or new age practices most likely you have given demons legal access to enter your life. The steps toward deliverance always start with repentance. Christ took the curse away by hanging on the Cross, taking all sin on Himself. Getting cleansed from spiritual defilement needs a determined heart. One needs to completely break with sin, idolatry, and malpractice and establish the truth of God's word on the inside.

Requirements to cast out demons.

1. Know and follow Jesus
2. Be filled with the Holy Spirit.
3. Have faith to take authority over evil spirits.

Faith-building Bible passages to study:

Matthew 4, Matthew 8:28-34, Matthew 9:32-33, Matthew 10:8, Matthew 12:22-30, Matthew 15:22-28, Matthew 17: 14-21, Mark 9:14-29, Luke 4:33-36, Acts 16:18.

Five steps to get free from demons.

1. Pray and fast. If needed, find someone or a deliverance ministry to stand with you in prayer.

2. Repent, turn from sin. Remove idols and ungodly items. Break with ungodly relationships if needed. Get rid of false religious artifacts, books, images, and pictures. Remove yourself from temptations or have them removed. Renounce all involvement in the above and decide to break with it for good.

3. Command evil spirits (by name if revealed) to leave you in Jesus' name. They must leave you now, they have no rights anymore to be there. Demons hate being cast out and will try to linger and tell you lies that you have no

authority to overpower them. Be persistent and firm and proclaim your freedom in Christ.

4. Ask the Holy Spirit to fill you and take every place where demons have left.

5. Keep the life-giving Christian habits of reading God's word, prayer, and obedience to God.

Recommended books for deliverance from demons and darkness

Derek Prince – They shall expel demons

Neil Anderson – Victory over darkness

Neil Anderson – The Bondage Breaker

Aliss Cresswell - Get Rid Of Those Demons: It's Your Time to Shine

Appendix B

Inner Healing

In the past twenty years, I have ministered the Lord's healing to many souls. It is not a public ministry, but one that has been hidden behind doors of safety and love. Where people can put their guard down, show their true emotions and just let it all out. Jesus never shames anyone for coming to Him with their pain. I have just been a vessel for Him; a listening ear, a mouthpiece to speak, His arms of love, and the hands to pass the tissues. Keeping trauma unhealed simply causes torment and anxiety. God is love and His love heals. There is no fear in His love. Shocking events like loss, accidents, childbirth, surgeries, abuse, abandonment, and neglect are all traumas that He can heal. But we will have to give Him access to our souls. The places where we have closed the doors, put up fences, or even build walls. I once suffered from what they call now post-traumatic stress syndrome. I had worked for six months in a former warzone and the aftermath of the war was still very present. It was a dangerous and depressing place with many hardships. I was a wreck when I got out. And I ran to other things until I got to know Jesus' care for my soul. I had kept a war zone diary and one day the Lord told me to burn the diary and bring all the hurt and pain I had carried to Him. I did what He told me to and then wept for a long time, letting all the pain out. No one understood what I had been through, but Jesus did. I used to have spirits appear to me at night, and would see terrible murder scenes in my dreams. As an Aid worker, you can't sit there and lose it. But when the Lord opened my heart and I let it all out, all the spirits and symptoms left!

Maybe you have been through a heartbreaking divorce. Perhaps you had an abusive parent. You might have had shocking events happen to you. Whatever the trauma has been in your life; Jesus wants to heal you right now. Here are the steps I take people through when they know they need inner healing.

Five steps to inner healing in Jesus

1. Recognize truth from lies. Jesus is the Truth, He wants to set you free. You don't have to carry the guilt or shame of your sins anymore. If anything happened outside of your own doing, you can ask Jesus to show you where He was when that happened. Or else invite Him into that terrible event in the past. Jesus is outside of time and so is the Cross. He can go there with you and take away your fears, your pain, your shame, and your guilt.

2. If you need to forgive anyone who has abused you, abandoned you, neglected you, hurt or harmed you; this is the time. When it seems hard to forgive someone for what they did to you, then it may help to think of that person differently. "Father forgive them, they know not what they do."

3. Let go of all grudges, resentment, and bitterness. Bring it to the Cross of Jesus Christ.

4. Receive now His love, mercy, forgiveness, grace, and healing, by releasing the pain, fear, and sorrow. Cry as long as you need to. Permit yourself to cry the tears you couldn't cry when you were in that situation. Let it all go and let it all out. Jesus is gentle and humble of heart and does not condemn you, my child. Be healed and be blessed!

5. Ask the Holy Spirit to fill up all the places where pain, rejection, and trauma have left.

Do you feel lighter and relieved? HalleluYah! God is so good! *"May the God of hope fill you with all joy and peace in believing that you may abound in hope by the power of the Holy Spirit." Romans 15:13*

Appendix C

Resource Guide

Encountering God through His Holy Spirit. Be equipped to Minister and do Jesus's works. Rob and Aliss have the best practical resources to disciple and train Christians to be active in the Ministry. Spirit Lifestyle – Rob and Aliss Cresswell – www.spiritlifestyle.com

If you need hands-on prayer for healing, on this website you can find any Healing Rooms nearby; Healing Rooms – John J. Lake – www.healingrooms.com

For foundational solid Bible teachings, go to; Derek Prince Ministries – www.derekprince.com

Specialized in deep complex trauma healing, including PTSD, please visit; Jim Banks House of Healing – www.jimandpatbanks.com

A comprehensive book on inner healing is called, The transformation of the inner man, written by veteran counselors; John and Paula Sandford.

Great books on Celtic Saints, Huguenots, and living in the Kingdom of God; Kathie Walters Ministry – www.kathiewaltersministry.com

Books about heroes of the Faith:
Rees Howells Intercessor – Norman Grubb
The Life Story of Lester Sumrall – Lester Sumrall
Wigglesworth, the complete story – Julian Wilson
The Hiding Place – Corrie ten Boom
John J. Lake, His Life, his sermons, his boldness of faith – KCP
Foxe's Book of martyrs – John Foxe

About the Author

Mirjam has been a missionary for about twenty years. She loves talking about the Kingdom of God and helping people find freedom in Christ.

Her passion is to see the people of God walk in the power of the Holy Spirit. She finds it her calling to raise up an Army of believers to conquer the earth for Christ.

Mirjam lives with her husband and son in Chattanooga, Tennessee. Besides home-making, ministry, and helping children, she likes to pioneer new things and use her creative abilities to reach people around the world.

Printed in June 2023
by Rotomail Italia S.p.A., Vignate (MI) - Italy